I0163889

The Great Secret

Robert Ott

Copyright © 2019 by Robert Ott

ISBN-13: 978-0-9890679-4-2

Library of Congress Control Number: 2019910564

To contact the author for questions and permissions:

ottrobert@aol.com

Introduction

I remember when it was the end of the second world war. My uncle, my mother's brother, was in the Hell On Wheels division in Germany. The news came on and said the war was over. Everybody on our street ran outside and cheered through their tears. I was not quite five years old, so I didn't fully understand, but I knew the war was over. I knew what was going on before because my father would put his Civil Defense helmet on when the air raid siren went on. He would go down to the corner and make sure everyone had house lights and headlights off.

I will never forget that day the war ended, I ran out with my Mother and stood under the cigar tree. I don't know the real name of the type of tree it was, but I remember it had long green pods on it that looked like cigars, so that's what I called it. There I was, a few months away from being five years old, standing under the cigar tree when Mrs. Frans, the neighbor, came out of her house and said, "Yes, it is great the war is over. But don't get too excited, because the next war is going to be with Communism."

It went through my mind...what is Communism? A few years later when I heard about the McCarthy hearings investigating Communists in the United States and in our own government, I was glued to our Muntz television. I would rush home from school, throw my books down, and fly into the living room to watch TV. I remember McCarthy asking everybody, "Are you a member of or have you ever been involved with the Communist party USA?"

I remember distinctly how everyone took the 5th. They would start out by pleading the fifth, yet, as it went on, they ended up routinely simply holding up five fingers instead of talking. I would see this and yell, "Mommy here is a Communist! Here is another Communist!"

In late 1962, I got a hold of a four page document called, "A Businessman Looks At Communism." The man who wrote it was from same state I was born in. At end of the document, there was a name to contact for more information: Dr. Schwartz and the Anti-Communist Crusade.

I joined Dr. Schwartz's crusade and read his newsletters. As he recommended, I spent the five dollars for *The Blue Book* from The John Birch Society. This was around the time that JFK was assassinated. I just could not believe that this could happen. Our President, assassinated on our own American soil.

By then I had gotten *The Blue Book* and I had read it over. I said, "Aw be durn, Robert Welch has the answer to my question of how could this happen." I decided at that point to join the John Birch Society. It was February of 1964.

Since that time, I have saved every book I have bought, every magazine and article, and I have built a massive library on my own. At this point, I have 2,000 books, magazines, and articles on what the Conspiracy is doing, what they've said, and what they are still doing and saying today.

I got on a political forum a number of years ago and mentioned Conspiracy and I was ripped up one side and down the other. I was told to prove there is a Conspiracy. I accepted that challenge. The result is this booklet you are holding. I hope you will find the subject as interesting and as informative as I have over the years.

The Conspiracy is alive and well. It is the driving force behind what is now being called "the Deep State." No matter what it is called, the facts have remained the same. The Communist party has many different circles like the ripple effect on water. The rock is the Conspiracy and the ripples are the groups of people they train. Each ripple trains the next one, all controlled by that rock at the center. The closer to the center, the more you know what is going on and what their goals are. The further out from center, the more the knowledge has dissipated, the more watered down the information is. In the distant ring in the water, one may not even believe there is a conspiracy because the further out you go, the less knowledge you have of the inner circle, the more brain washed you get as each ripple gives orders to the next and out it goes. It just keeps blooming out. A conspiracy has to work in secret, but it is still controlled by the nucleus, the center of the Conspiracy. They pull the strings on the Deep State.

You will find out what that center is and what their goals are for our Republic and real Americans as you read this book.

The Great Secret

During May 2009, I was challenged by some people on a forum to present some evidence of a master conspiracy to enslave the world. They did not believe in one, but they could not present any facts to support their belief. The Insiders are so sure that they now have a "slam-dunk" with regard to achieving their goal, that they are very open with what they are doing. Today their plans are not so much a secret, except with one major group – the Bilderberg Group.

In my lifetime, I have studied and accumulated a library of information on the Conspiracy and its goals for World domination. The information I have provided here in *The Great Secret* does not have formal in-text citations because it was not intended for publication. Yet, I have found myself with an offer to publish. For the sake of getting the word out there, I have agreed. I have included a general Works Cited section at the end of this book for your further reading of the source material. Please know that the facts, quotes, historical accuracies, and information I have drawn upon here have been taken from a large number of sources that are in my library which I have collected through my history studies since November, 1963.

A lack of evidence of a master conspiracy is not the problem. The problem is dealing with such vast, cumbersome, and time-consuming research material. There are mountains of evidence, which can be broken down into three categories: primary source material, consisting of original documents, diaries, records, and correspondence from persons directly involved in the events; contemporary source accounts written about the events close to the time they occurred; and secondary source materials. The major problem with secondary source materials is if it does not contain verifiable primary or contemporary sources, it becomes only the opinion of the author. My research deals with primary and contemporary material. I will only give an overview of some of the evidence. Since May, 2009, I have updated this paper twice with more current evidence of the master plan to march the people of the earth into a one world government, also known as a New World Order.

This master conspiracy had its start in Bavaria, Germany, and was founded on May 1, 1776, by Adam Weishaupt, a professor of Cannon Law at the University of Ingolstadt. It was called the Order of the Illuminati.

The original published form of the Order's papers was divided into two separate titles and published in the same year, 1787, in Munich. Published collections of the Illuminati papers have been reprinted by: Richard van Dulmen, ed., Stuttgart-Bad Cannstatt, 1977; and Henry Coston, Paris, 1979. Two works that utilized the original documents were: John Robison's *Proofs of a Conspiracy*, NY, 1798, the first page stating: "Conspiracy [. . .] carried on in the secret meetings of Free Masons, Illuminati and Reading Societies."; and Abbe Augustine Barruel's massive 4 vols. *Memoirs Illustrating the History of Jacabinism*, London, 1797-1798.

One might ask, if the Order was secret, how were the original papers published? A courier sent from Frankfurt to Paris in 1785 was killed by a bolt of lightning. Papers were found on him about the Order along with the name Xavier Zwack. When the authorities raided Zwack's home, his copy of Weishaupt's writings were found. In those writings are found detailed instructions for fomenting hatred and bloodshed between different racial, religious, and ethnic groups. Hatred among children and their parents was introduced. Even instructions about the kinds of buildings to be burned in urban insurrections. In these papers are found the tactics used by 21st Century subversives. James H. Billington, former Librarian of Congress, states in his extensive 1980 study *The Origins of the Revolutionary Faith,* "it is from Bavarian Illuminism that the modern revolutionary tradition descends."

Adam Weishaupt stated in his papers that: "These [ruling] powers are despots when they do not conduct themselves by its [the Orders] principles; and it is therefore our duty to surround them with its members, so that the profane may have no access to them. Thus we are able most powerfully to promote its [the Order's] interests."

As written in his papers, Weishaupt's two chief doctrines were anarchism and pantheism. These are the attack on property and legitimate civil authority, and the attack on the Judeo-Christian God, organized religion, and objective morality.

The research done by Robison revealed that Weishaupt had long been scheming the establishment of an Association or Order, which in time should govern the world. In the Manifesto of 1794, issued by the Duke of Brunswick (a conspirator who had a change of heart) states that, "it would be a crime against truth and humanity to leave any longer shrouded in a veil [. . .] a great sect which, taking for its motto the good and the happiness of man, worked in the darkness of the conspiracy to make the happiness of humanity a prey for itself."

In the research of Abbe Barruel, we find this warning, "You thought the revolution ended in France, and the Revolution in France was only the first attempt of the Jacobins. In the desires of a terrible and formidable sect, you have only reached the first stage of the plans it has formed for that general Revolution which is to overthrow all the thrones, all the alters, annihilate all property, efface all law, and end by dissolving all society."

In his original papers, Weishaupt tells us that, "Princes and nations shall vanish from the earth. The human race will then become one family." It is through this that "freedom for the world" will be regained by making the world "fit to govern itself...." And he states: "This is our Great Secret."

By 1815, the Order grew, and was divided into two groups: Sublime Perfect Masters and Society of the Seasons. These two groups eventually formed the League of the Just, which commissioned Karl Marx to write *The Communist Manifesto*. After its publication, they changed their name to the Communist League. Frederic Engles wrote in the 1888 Preface to the English edition, "The Manifesto was published as the platform of the Communist League, [...which was] before 1848 unavoidably a secret society." In the Preface to the 1872 German edition, we find that: "The Communist League, [. . .] which could of course be only a secret one [. . .] commissioned the undersigned [i.e.., Marx & Engles], to draw up for publication a detailed theoretical and practical program of the party. Such was the origin of the following Manifesto." Therefore; in their own words, communism was handed down through this secret society. Their goal remains the same today as it was over 200 years ago – a one world ruled by a master elite. As verified by James P. Warburg, a backer of the United World Federalists, who once told the US Senate Foreign Relations Committee, "We shall have world government whether we like or not. The question is only whether world government will be achieved by consent or by conquest."

In 1884, Pope Leo XIII (Vincenzo Pecci) issued the document, *Humanum Genus*, in which he makes it clear that the system of Adam Weishaupt had expanded, "organized bodies which, though differing in name, are nevertheless so bound together." He tells us that they remain secret so as to hide from the public, and from many of their members, "their secret and final designs, the names of the chief leaders, and certain secret and inner meetings, as well as their decisions, and the ways and means of carrying them out." What was their goal? Leo XIII tells us that it was the complete overthrow of the "whole religious and political order of the world...and the substitution of a new state of things."

While running for the presidency in 1912, Woodrow Wilson delivered a speech on October 19 in Carnegie Hall, in which he remarked: "Since I entered politics, I have chiefly had men's views confided to me privately. Some of the biggest men in the United States, in the field of commerce and manufacturing, are afraid of somebody, are afraid of something. They know that there is a power somewhere so organized, so subtle, so watchful, so interlocked, so complete, so pervasive, that they had better not speak above their breath when they speak in condemnation of it." And twenty years later, President

Franklin Roosevelt wrote to Col. Edward M. House (President Wilson's chief adviser) on November 21, 1933 that "The real truth of the matter is, as you and I know, that a financial element in the larger centers has owned the Government ever since the days of Andrew Jackson."

In 1917, the Bolshevik or Russian Revolution was financed by the international bankers like the Rothschilds, Rockefellers, Schiffs, Warburgs, Harrimans and Milers. Many of these same banking families secretly financed Hitler and continue to finance both sides of conflicts in order to establish their world government and profit (money and power) from it in the process.

Winston Churchill, before he was Prime Minister of Great Britain, was aware of the roots of the Communist Revolution. He wrote in the February 18th, 1920 issue of the *London Illustrated Sunday Herald* that, "From the days of Spartacus (Spartacus was the code name of the Illuminati founder and leader Adam Weishaupt) to those of Karl Marx, to those of Trotsky, Bella Kuhn, Rose Luxembourg, and Emma Goldman, this world-wide conspiracy has been steadily growing." He affirmed, "It has been the mainspring of every subversive movement during the 19th century; and now at last, this band of extraordinary personalities from the underworld of the great cities of Europe and America have gripped the Russian people by the hair of their heads and have become practically undisputed masters of that enormous empire."

Dr. Carroll Quigley was a professor at the Foreign Service School of Georgetown University, he formally taught at Princeton and Harvard and did research in the archives of

France, Italy, and England. He is the author of the widely known text, *Evolution of Civilization*. This is the same Professor that Bill Clinton paid tribute to during his 1992 acceptance speech at the Democratic Party Convention. It is Quigley's book, *Tragedy and Hope: A History of the World In Our Time*, 1966, that is the most current authoritative source regarding the master conspiracy. Why? Quigley tells us, "I know of the operations of this network because I have studied it for twenty years and was permitted for two years, in the early 1960's, to examine its papers and secret records." He has "no aversion to it," but has a "difference of opinion" with it because "it wishes to remain unknown, and I believe its role in history is significant enough to be known." That is his reason for writing his 1,348 page book.

Throughout his massive book, he assures us that we can trust these well-meaning men who are secretly operating behind the scenes. Quigley considers himself not only an insider, but a member of the intellectual elite among the insiders. He believes that the forces of total global control are now sufficiently entrenched, so that they can reveal their true identity without fear of being successfully overturned. This was confirmed by the top elitist, David Rockefeller, who in June 1991, at a Bilderberg Group meeting at Sand, Germany, said that he was "grateful to the *Washington Post, The New York Times, Time* magazine and other publications for not printing what went on at the group's meetings. It would have been impossible for us to develop our plan for the world if we had been subject to the bright lights of publicity during these years. But the world is now more sophisticated and prepared to march towards a world government." He went on to condemn national sovereignty, "The supranational sovereignty of an intellectual elite and world bankers is surely preferable to the national autodetermination practiced in the past centuries."

Rockefeller in his 2002 *Memoirs,* stated, "For more than a century ideological extremists [. . .] attack the Rockefeller family for the inordinate influence they claim we wield over American political and economic institutions. Some even believe we are part of a secret cabal working against the best interests of the United States, characterizing my family and me as 'internationalists' and of conspiring with others around the world to build a more integrated global political and economic structure – one world, if you will. If that's the charge, I stand guilty, and I am proud of it."

Carroll Quigley expresses contempt for those who thought the Communist conspiracy was the real center of collectivized conspiracy. He ridicules their conclusions and then turns around and admits that their conclusions were correct – American anti-Communists had merely erred in knowing whom to blame, "There does exist, and has existed for a generation, an international Anglophile network which operates, to some extent, in the way the radical Right believes the Communists act. In fact, this network, which we may identify as the Round Table Groups, has no aversion to cooperating with the Communists, or any other groups, and frequently does so."

Dr. Bella Dodd, a former member of the National Committee of the US Communist Party, made this statement: "I think the Communist conspiracy is merely a branch of a much bigger conspiracy." She became aware of this right after WW II when the Communist Party USA (CPUSA) had difficulty getting instructions from Moscow. She said that the top leaders of the CPUSA were told that any time they needed an immediate answer on a problem to contact any one of three designated persons at the Waldorf Towers. She noted that whatever answer any one of these three men gave, Moscow always ratified them. These men were neither Russian nor communists. Dr. Dodd said, "I would certainly like to find out who is really running things."

Carroll Quigley tells of the next evolution of the conspiracy – Cecil Rhodes' secret society, "In this secret society Rhodes was to be the leader." He goes on to name the ones who were in the inner and the outer circles of this, The Society of the Elect, established March, 1891. Later to be known as the Round Table Groups.

Cecil Rhodes' long-range program was "to federate the English-speaking peoples and to bring all the habitable portions of the world under their control." Rhodes would write to his associate, William Stead, "The only feasible [way] to carry this idea out is a secret [society] gradually absorbing the wealth of the world." Rhodes described this as "a scheme to take the government of the whole world."

After 1914, it became apparent that the society needed to be greatly extended. Lionel Curtis was given this task. He established two fronts for the Round Table Group: in London, England it was the Royal Institute of International Affairs (RIIA), founded in 1922, official publication, *International Affairs*; and in the US, the Council on Foreign Relations (CFR), founded in 1921, which was also a front for J.P. Morgan & Co., CFR's official publication, *Foreign Affairs*. Quigley also gives the names of the original conspirators and the media that they control.

A third arm, a parent organization of the CFR, was established in 1925, called the Institute of Pacific Relations (IPR). The Senate Committee on the Judiciary, declared in 1952: "The Institute of Pacific Relations was a vehicle used by the Communists to orient American Far Eastern policies toward Communist objectives." The report said that the "core of officials and staff members who controlled IPR were either Communist or pro-Communist."

In P.E. Corbett's *Post-War Worlds*, 1942, published under the auspices of the leftist Institute of Pacific Relations, one reads that "A world association binding together the coordinating regional groupings of states may evolve toward one universal federal government, as in the past loose confederations have grown into federal unions." In other words, to achieve a World Federal Government, one might first perform an "end run" of forming "regional economic entities, like the current European Union, ASEAN, and NAFTA (North American Free Trade Agreement). Political union will be much easier to accomplish after the economies of nations within regional grouping have become almost inextricably intertwined.

Douglas Farah is closely associated with the CFR, the US arm of the powerful Bilderberg Group, and the Hudson Institute. The Hudson Institute "has done more to shape the way Americans react to political and social events, think, vote, and generally conduct themselves in perhaps any [way] except [for] the kingpin of the brainwashing establishment Tavistock Institute of Human Relations itself." Hudson primarily specializes in defense policy research and relations with Russia.

The CFR boasts a membership of around 5,000. But its roster includes literally hundreds of powerful figures occupying key positions in the media – not merely writers, reporters and news anchors, but also editors, publishers, and executives who define what news is, and how it is covered. Just as significantly, the tiny CFR clique has for decades been the power and decision-maker behind the executive branch of the US government, as well as much of academia.

Investigative author James Perloff in 2009 noted, "Since the Council's founding in 1921, 21 secretaries of defense or war, 19 secretaries of the treasury, 17 secretaries of state, and 15 CIA directors have hailed from the Council on Foreign Relations." The CFR's dominant influence extends to both Democratic and Republican administrations.

Carroll Quigley states that the financial goal of the CFR is "nothing less than to create a world system of financial control in private hands able to dominate the political system of each country and the economy of the world as a whole."

In his October 30, 1993, "Ruling Class Journalists" essay, *Washington Post* journalist Richard Harwood candidly discussed how the CFR dominates our news media. Harwood described the CFR as, "the closest thing we have to a ruling establishment in the United States [. . . .] Its members are the people who for more than half a century have managed our international affairs and our military-industrial complex." After listing the executive-branch positions then occupied by CFR members, Harwood continued, "For what is distinctly modern about the council these days, is the considerable involvement of journalists and other media figures who account for more than 10% of the membership."

"The editorial page editor, the deputy editorial page editor, executive editor, managing editor, foreign editor, national affairs editor, business and financial editor, and various writers as well as [now deceased] Katharine Graham, the paper's principle owner, represents the *Washington Post* in the council's membership," observed Harwood. That makes one wonder if the CFR was the reason Katharine Graham was the first woman to run a nationally prominent newspaper in the US, served as publisher from 1969 to 1979 and headed The Washington Post Company into the early 1990s as chairman of the board and CEO. Harwood described the CFR representations among the owners, management, editorial personnel of the other media giants *New York Times, Wall Street Journal, Los Angeles Times,* ABC, CBS, NBC and many others. These media heavyweights "do not merely analyze and interpret foreign policy for the United States, they help make it," he concluded. Rather than offering an independent perspective on our ruler's actions, the Establishment media act as the ruling elite's voice, conditioning the public to accept and even embrace insider designs that otherwise might not be politically attainable.

Admiral Chester Ward, a member of the CFR for 16 years, resigned in disgust when he realized that the CFR's agenda is to promote "disarmament and submergence of United States sovereignty and national independence into an all-powerful one-world government." He also charged that the "Lust to surrender the sovereignty and independence of the United States is pervasive throughout most of the membership. The majority visualize the utopian submergence of the United States as a subsidiary administration unit of a global government."

Carroll Quigley confirmed in his book what Admiral Ward said of the CFR: "The Council on Foreign Relations is the American Branch of a society which originated in England" and "believes national boundaries should be obliterated and one-world rule established."

Another one to confirm the CFR's agenda is CFR President Richard Haass when he said, "states must be prepared to cede some sovereignty to world bodies if the international system is to function. All of this suggests that sovereignty must be redefined if states are to cope with globalization. At its core, globalization entails the increasing volume, velocity, and importance of flows — within and across borders — of people, ideas, greenhouse gases, goods, dollars, drugs, viruses, e-mails, weapons and a good deal else, challenging one of sovereignty's fundamental principles: the ability to control what crosses borders in either direction."

The Royal Institute of International Affairs (RIIA) also has an important role in the formation of a world state, and planning it in "out of the way places and with little ado." In a 1931 address, select globalists in Copenhagen, Denmark. RIIA staff leader Arnold J. Toynbee literally denounced national sovereignty: "I will merely repeat that we are at present working, discreetly but with all our might, to wrest this mysterious political force called sovereignty out of the clutches of the local national states of our world. And all the time we are denying with our lips what we are doing with our hands." What they are doing is building a New World Order.

According to Haass and the CFR, the only answer to this predicament is a progressive weakening of national sovereignty and a steady move to global government. "Globalization thus implies that sovereignty is not only becoming weaker in reality, but that it needs to become weaker," says Haass. "States would be wise to weaken sovereignty in order to protect themselves, because they cannot insulate themselves from what goes on elsewhere. Sovereignty is no longer a sanctuary."

Haass opines that, "Our notion of sovereignty must therefore be conditional, even contractual, rather than absolute." Which means that our Constitution, which specifically defines and limits the powers of the U.S. federal government, would be completely conditional, at the whim of those who are defining of what our sovereignty consists.

"The goal," says Haass, "should be to redefine sovereignty for the era of globalization, to find a balance between a world of fully sovereign states and an international system of either world government or anarchy."

World government or anarchy — those are our only options, according to the CFR luminaries. During the decades of the 1960s through the 1990s, the internationalists muted their calls for world government, preferring fuzzier labels such as "international law," "the rule of law," and "interdependence" to avoid generating the popular alarm that a transparent attempt to subject U.S. citizens to UN rule would engender.

We have more than a hint of the world government plan in the title of the CFR Issue Brief, "The Global Climate Change Regime."

"Regime" is a term the globalists would not likely have used even a couple of decades ago, because that would have been a dead giveaway as to where they want to take us. The word regime is defined as: a "mode of rule or management," "a form of government (a socialist regime)," or "a government in power."

We get another substantial hint from the CFR webpage hosting the "The Global Climate Change Regime," which notes that it is part of the CFR's "multimedia Global Governance Monitor from the International Institutions and Global Governance program."

Jacques Attali, a committed world government proponent and an advisor to former President Nicolas Sarkozy of France, flatly stated in 2008: "Global governance is just a euphemism for global government."

Over the past two decades, the CFR journal *Foreign Affairs* has published numerous articles hyping the global-warming non-crisis, and its fellows and members have fright-peddled the anthropogenic global warming scare stories in countless editorials and interviews in the major (CFR-dominated) media. The Council's many task forces, panels, and speaker programs have pumped the false alarms of melting polar caps and rising sea levels to influential opinion molders, policymakers, and legislators. On a global scale, the CFR influences an even wider audience of opinion molders, policymakers, and legislators through its Council of Councils, an important adjunct of the CFR's International Institutions and Global Governance (IIGG) program. The Council of Councils is a formal association of 25 of the CFR's "sister" organizations. These include: Canada's Center for International Governance Innovation; the French Institute of International Relations; the German Institute for International and Security Affairs; Italy's Institute of International Affairs; the Polish Institute of International Affairs; and, of course, Britain's The Royal Institute of International Affairs (RIIA), also known as Chatham House.

Jim Garrison, President of the Gorbachev Foundation, USA, in 1995 stated, "Over the next 20 to 30 years, we are going to end up with world government. It's inevitable; [w]e have to empower the United Nations and [. . .] we have to govern and regulate human interaction."

In the inaugural issue of *Foreign Affairs* (Sept. 1922), is found an article condemning "safety first" and "America first." An article in the second issue (Dec. 1922) declared: "Obviously there is going to be no peace for mankind so long as it remains divided into fifty or sixty independent states." What is needed is, "some kind of international system [. . .] which will put an end to the attempt of every nation to make itself secure. The real problem today is that of world government."

In 1974, *Foreign Affairs* carried an article by Richard N. Gardner (CFR), "The Hard Road to World Order." He states that "the house of world order will have to be built from the bottom up rather than from the top down." He explained that "an end run around national sovereignty, eroding it piece by piece, will accomplish much more than the old-fashioned frontal assault."

In the early 20th century, the words "propaganda" and "war" became synonymous with one another, thanks to the efforts of two men – Walter Lippmann, the most influential political commentator of his time, and Edward Bernays, Sigmund Freud's nephew. Bernays was one of the founders of the field of public relations, which was opinion-manipulation techniques. In 1928, he wrote in his book, *Propaganda*, "It was of course the astounding success propaganda during the [First World] War that opened the eyes of the intell [. . . .] We are governed, our minds are molded, our tastes formed, our ideas suggested, largely by men we have never heard of. Whatever attitude one chooses to take toward this condition, it remains a fact that almost every act of our daily lives, whether in the sphere of politics or business, our social conduct or our ethical thinking, we are dominated by a relatively small number of persons, a trifling fraction of our hundred and twenty million [US citizens at that time] who understand the mental processes and social patterns of the masses. It is they who pull the wires which control the public mind and who harness old social forces and contrive new ways to bind and guide the world."

Walter Lippmann and Edward Bernays participated in a secret study on the effects of manipulating war information for the purposes of mobilizing mass support for the war. The study was sponsored by the Royal Institute for International Affairs, also known as the Chatham House. It serves the same purpose as the CFR, to give the conspiracy a needed presence in Europe and the US.

Researchers discovered that less than 10% of people understand that the process of reasoning requires the ability to observe a problem without immediately passing judgment on it. Since then, the brain washers have used this fact to control war and important issues in society in general. In 1991, over 87% of Americans wanted Saddam Hussein's head on a platter during their support behind the first gulf war. But in 1990, 90% of Americans could not pinpoint Iraq on a map, and 80% didn't even know who Saddam was.

"In this manner," writes John Coleman, in *Conspirators' Hierarchy: The Story of the Committee of 300*, "irrationality is elevated to a high level of public consciousness. The manipulators then play upon this to undermine and distract the grasp of reality governing any given situation and, the more complex the problems of a modern industrial society became, the easier it became to ring greater and greater distractions to ear so that what we ended up with was that the absolutely inconsequential opinions of masses of people, created by skilled manipulators, assumed the position of scientific fact."

At the Tavistock Institute, Coleman says, "Eric Trist and Frederick Emery developed a theory of 'social turbulence'," a so-called "softening up effect of future shocks" – which means a population could be softened up through mass phenomena such as energy shortages, climate change, economic and financial collapse, or terrorist attacks. "If the 'shocks' were to come close enough to each other, and if they were delivered within increasing intensity, then it was possible to drive the entire society into a state of mass psychosis," claimed Trist and Emery. They also stated that "individuals would become disassociated, as they tried to flee from the terror of the shocking, emerging reality; people would withdraw into a state of denial, retreating into popular entertainments and diversions, while being prone to outbursts of rage."

What Trist and Emery were talking about is the two sides of the same coin – on one side, guiding the covert, subtle manipulation and control of thought and human consciousness through the power of media. "On the other side," wrote the pseudonymous John Quinn, for *News-Hawk* on-line, on October 10, 1999, "directly and overtly shifting the paradigm, changing the basic concepts, widening the parameters, and changing the playing field and all the rules of play by which society defines itself within an exceptionally short period of time."

As Paul McGuire has said, "The destruction of the American economy and the dollar did not happen by accident. It was a planned event, like the euro and other currencies around the world." There are no food shortages, energy crisis, or man-made global warming. All of this, and more that we hear every day, is manufactured crises that have been created to bring about a world government.

The week of April 15, 1945, Alger Hiss, working for the State Department, was named the Secretary-General for the San Francisco conference of the soon-to-be United Nations. Hiss was not only the active Secretary-General at the San Francisco conference, but also served on the steering and executive committees which were charged with the responsibilities of actually writing the new UN's charter. In such a position, he had a tremendous amount of influence on the drafting of the charter itself. He was later to be identified as a Soviet Agent within the United States government. There were 43 other members of the US Delegation to the San Francisco conference who were or would later become members of the Council on Foreign Relations.

The UN Universal Declaration of Human Rights adopted by the General Assembly of Paris in 1948 grants all sorts of human rights in its early articles and emasculates them with this language in Article 29: "In the exercise of his rights and freedoms, everyone should be subject only to such limitations as are determined by law solely for the purpose of securing recognition and respect for the rights and freedoms of others and of meeting the just requirements of morality, public order, and the general welfare in a democratic society. These rights and freedoms may in no case be exercised contrary to the purposes and principles of the United Nations."

Even Adlai Stevenson admitted that, "Every one of the main charter restrictions has been loosened," and speculated, "I suspect that if in 1945 there had been proposed such a world organization endowed with all the actual authority, and energy which the U.N. is showing today, the nations would never have agreed to it." And, John Foster Dulles (member of the CFR) claimed, "I have never seen any proposal made for collective security with 'teeth' in it, or for 'world government' or for 'world federation,' which could not be carried out either by the United Nations or under the United Nations Charter." And that comes from a person who was one of the UN's former Secretary of founders.

Dulles also recognized the revolutionary role of the UN in the gradual drive toward world government. "The United Nations," he wrote, "represents not a final stage in the development of world order, but only a primitive stage. Therefore its primary task is to create the conditions which will make possible a more highly developed organization."

One of the UN's specialized agencies actively working to create those conditions is UNESCO. On one occasion in the UN's early years, when UNESCO was widely criticized for promoting One World propaganda, the *Saturday Review* candidly editorialized: "If UNESCO is attacked on the grounds that it is helping to prepare the world's people for world government, then it is an error to burst forth with apologetic statements and denials. Let us face it: the job of UNESCO is to help create and promote the elements of world citizenship. When faced with such a 'charge,' let us by all means affirm it from the housetops."

Another plan in the drive toward a world government is "sustainable development" another name for *Agenda 21,* which describes a plan in which the UN, acting as custodian of the planet, would regulate all human activity. This was aptly described by Divid Sitarz, editor of the authoritative version of *Agenda 21: "*Effective execution of *Agenda 21* will require a profound reorientation of all human society, unlike anything the world has ever experienced – a major shift in the priorities of both governments and individuals and an unprecedented redeployment of human and financial resources. This shift will demand that a concern for the environmental consequences of every human action be integrated into individual and collective decision-making at every level." This will require active participation, as Sitarz states, "by farmers and consumers, by legislators, by scientists, by women, by children – in short, by *every person on Earth.*"

The Law of the Sea Treaty (LOST) is yet another major grab for world domination by the UN.

The following phrases, underlined in the preamble to LOST, show that the US will have no say in how the oceans are used: "Bearing in mind that the achievement of these goals will contribute to the realization of a just and equitable international economic order which takes into account the interests and needs of mankind as a whole and, in particular, the special interests and needs of developing countries, whether coastal or land-locked [. . . .]" "Desiring by this Convention to develop the principles embodied in resolution 2749 (XXV) of 17 December 1970, in which the General Assembly of the United Nations solemnly declared *inter alia* that the area of the seabed and ocean floor and the subsoil thereof, beyond the limits of national jurisdiction, as well as its resources, are the common heritage of mankind, the exploration and exploitation of which shall be carried out for the benefit of mankind as a whole, irrespective of the geographical location of States." The key words, here are: "international economic order," in which the UN seeks the redistribution of natural, financial, and technological resources; "mankind as a whole," "common heritage of mankind," and "benefit of mankind," which means the UN seeks to globalize Marx's formula, "from each according to his ability, to each according to his needs." As columnist William Norman Grigg worded it, "What's mine is mine, what's yours is ours."

Article 2 states, "The sovereignty over the territorial sea [200 nautical miles from a nation's coast] is exercised subject to this Convention and to other rules of international law." Under LOST, a nation's sovereignty over its coastal water would be controlled by the UN.

Article 137 states that, "No State shall claim or exercise sovereignty or sovereign rights over any part of the Area [70% of the earth's surface] or its resources, nor shall any State or natural or juridical person appropriate any part thereof. No such claim or exercise of sovereignty or sovereign rights nor such appropriation shall be recognized," and "No State or natural or juridical person shall claim, acquire or exercise rights with respect to the minerals recovered from the Area except in accordance with this Part. Otherwise, no such claim, acquisition or exercise of such rights shall be recognized."

Article 144 explains the transfer of technology. "The Authority [created by the UN] shall take measures in accordance with this Convention: to acquire technology and scientific knowledge relating to activities in the Area [70% of earth's surface]; and to promote and encourage the transfer to developing States of such technology and scientific knowledge so that all States Parties benefit there from."

Article 150 states, "participation in revenues by the Authority and the transfer of technology to the Enterprise [created by the UN] and developing States as provided for in this Convention."

Articles 207(4) and 208(5) set the stage for the eventual control by the UN over our inland waterways. Our federal government has helped out the UN with its eventual control over our inland waterways by establishing the White Water to Blue Water Initiative (WW2BW), which the State Department and The National Oceanic and Atmospheric Administration describe as a "sustainable development partnership" in the form of "an international alliance" of government agencies, UN connected bodies, and radical environmental groups.

Under LOST, the US will not have veto power as in the Security Council – but, rather, in LOST, the US will have only one vote among 193 nations.

Singapore's Tommy Koh, the president of the Third UN Conference on the Law of the Sea, stated in 2002, that LOST is "a comprehensive constitution for the ocean" covering "every aspect of the uses and the resources of the sea."

The UN itself admitted how radical LOST is in a document celebrating the 25th anniversary of the treaty's completion: "The United Nations Convention on the Law of the Sea … is perhaps one of the most significant but less recognized

20th century accomplishments in the arena of international law…. Its scope is vast: it covers all ocean space, with all its uses, including navigation and over flight; all uses of all its resources, living and nonliving, on the high seas, on the ocean floor and beneath, on the continental shelf and in the territorial seas; the protection of the marine environment; and basic law and order…. The Convention is widely recognized by the international community as the legal framework within which all activities in the ocean and the seas must be carried out."

Former UN Secretary-General U Thant praised founding Soviet dictator V.I. Lenin in 1970, saying that Lenin's "ideals of peace and peaceful coexistence [. . .] are in line with the aims of the UN Charter." Just in case one forgot, Lenin's concept of "peace" was world socialism, secured through terror and subversion.

For those of you who read George Orwell's famous book *1984*, do you remember thinking that the Party's slogan "War is Peace" was too ridiculous to actually be believed by anyone? BUT TODAY we have a United Nations "peace" army that is out waging peace on almost a dozen nations thanks to our own government. Now we have Orwell's "perpetual war for perpetual peace."

The United Nations' Rio+20 conference that concluded on the 22 of June, 2012, was not about saving the planet from environmental devastation or about eradicating poverty.

Instead, Lord Monckton said it was about shackling the planet under a global government. Monckton, who attended the conference, has served as policy advisor to Margaret

Thatcher when she was Prime Minister of Great Britain. At Rio+20 Monckton noted, "They were still effectively talking about mechanization for setting up a global government so that they could shut down the West, shut down democracy, and bring freedom to an end worldwide."

The 57th secret meeting of the Bilderberg Group occurred on May 14-17, 2009, in Greece. Investigative author Daniel Estulin states that he obtained a copy of the pre-meeting book sent out to attendees that presents a two option economic discussion: "Either a prolonged, agonizing depression that dooms the world to decades of stagnation, decline and poverty [. . .] or an intense-but-shorter depression that paves the way for a new sustainable economic world order, with less sovereignty but more efficiency." If this plan comes to fruition, it will be the demise of our Bill of Rights and our independence. We will be granted our rights by an all-powerful world government that can and will remove those rights at any time they see fit.

Each year since 2013, the World Government Summit (WGS) has had high profile dignitaries in attendance as was the case on February 10-12, 2019, with over 4,000 attendees from more than 150 countries that were attending the WGS in Dubai. The WGS sister group with its own yearly conference in Davos Switzerland is the World Economic Forum (WEF). Its website states that it is "a global platform dedicated to shaping the future of governments worldwide." Each year the summit sets the agenda for the next generation of governments. Have you ever wondered why you do not hear or read about these two groups? Let a true internationalist tell us what these two groups are up to, one Michael Hirst, a senior correspondent for *Foreign Policy* magazine, stated, "The internationalists were always hard at work in quiet places making plans for a more perfect global community. In the end, the internationalists have always dominated national policy. Even so, they haven't bragged about their globe-building for fear of reawakening the other half of the American psyche, our berserker nativism. If so, they have always done it in the most out of the way places and with little ado." This comes from a special "Devos edition" of *Newsweek* for December 2001 through February 2002, which was intended for only the elite attending the WGS in Davos.

In another admission of their plans for a world government, the first point Hirst makes was about a group named the Inquiry, who secretly met in New York in Dec 1917 to draw up Wilson's Fourteen Points which included the formation of the League of Nations, which was the first effort at a world government. The next step he talked about was in 1944; it was during that time that they formed the IMF and the world bank. A year later, the United Nations came to life. Hirst stated, "So what emerged took us more or less by surprise. We had built a global order without quite realizing it, bit by bit, error by error."

What is advocated at these conferences, as any American attending them would notice, is nothing short of outright treason. Hirst insists in that special edition of *Newsweek,* "we must now embrace the global community we ourselves built" – when he uses the phrases "we must" and "we ourselves built," he is telling us that the American people must accept what these one worlders have built because they are so much more knowledgeable than the common person. What must we accept? The world government that would entirely wipe out our Constitution. We would be so-called slaves to these "wise men."

In a September 21, 2013, article, *Salon*, entitled "Elites' Strange Plot to take over the World," Matt Stoller writes, "as liberals gently chuckle at right-wing paranoia about what they perceive as an imagined plot to create a world government, it is the conservatives who have a more accurate read on history. There was a serious plan to get rid of American sovereignty in favor of a globalist movement, and the various institutions the right wing hates – the IMF, the World Bank, the U.N. – were seen as stepping stones to it." He goes on to note, "institutional framework of a world government composed of Western European and American states remains far more potent than we like to imagine, even beyond the security apparatus revealed by Snowden's documents. For example, in every major free trade agreement since NAFTA, U.S. courts have been subordinated to international tribunals, which operate according to rules laid out by the World Trade Organization." He goes on to say that the federal reserve "became the central banker to the world." The global elites push onward to a global solution.

In *The New American* magazine of April 8, 2019, is an article entitled "The War on Sovereignty" written by William F. Jasper where he states, "One measure to the effectiveness of their propaganda is the mere mention of world government, new world order, Agenda 21/Agenda 2030, or dozens of other related subjects is enough to put one beyond the pale, triggering eye rolls, sneers, and exasperated sighs from those who are conditioned to believe such things don't exist, or can be explained benignly." I do hope for those of you who are reading this, you don't fall under any of those categories.

It has been said history teaches by analogy, not identity. The historical experience is not one of staying in the present and looking back. Rather it is one of going back into the past and returning to the present with a wider and more intense consciousness of the restrictions of our former outlook.

History is also a story of conflict between good and evil. It is not a series of accidents, it is planned by people for good or evil purposes. As Paul McGuire has said, "The destruction of the American economy and the dollar did not happen by accident. It was a planned event, like the euro and other currencies around the world." There are no food shortages, energy crises, or man-made global warming. All of this and more that we hear every day is manufactured crises that have been created to bring about a world government.

Either we start re-writing history through that great blinding light of truth – or we plunge into the abyss of darkness and slavery. It can be stopped with the truth of light shining on it, because that is one thing that will dissolve a conspiracy – the truth. As was said many years ago, "Is life so dear, or peace so sweet, as to be purchased at the price of chains and slavery?" You must make that decision for yourself as to which you are going to choose.

God Bless America

ADDENDUM
ONE

Congressional Record—Appendix, pp. A34-A35
Current Communist Goals

EXTENSION OF REMARKS OF HON. A. S. HERLONG, JR.
OF FLORIDA IN THE HOUSE OF REPRESENTATIVES

Thursday, January 10, 1963

Mr. HERLONG. Mr. Speaker, Mrs. Patricia Nordman of
De Land, Fla., is an ardent and articulate opponent of
communism, and until recently published the De Land
Courier, which she dedicated to the purpose of alerting the
public to the dangers of communism in America.

At Mrs. Nordman's request, I include in the RECORD,
under unanimous consent, the following "Current
Communist Goals," which she identifies as an excerpt from
"The Naked Communist," by Cleon Skousen: (These goals
included):

CURRENT COMMUNIST GOALS

-- U.S. acceptance of coexistence as the only alternative to
atomic war.

-- U.S. willingness to capitulate in preference to engaging
in atomic war.

-- Develop the illusion that total disarmament [by] the
United States would be a demonstration of moral strength.

-- Permit free trade between all nations regardless of
Communist affiliation and regardless of whether or not

items could be used for war. (Karl Marx was for free trade in the sense that it is being proposed today: "[Free Trade] breaks up old nationalities ... In a word, the free trade system hastens the social revolution." – Karl Marx, Brussels, Belgium, January 9, 1848.)

-- Provide American aid to all nations regardless of Communist domination.

-- Promote the U.N. as the only hope for mankind. If its charter is rewritten, demand that it be set up as a one-world government with its own independent armed forces.

-- Resist any attempt to outlaw the Communist Party.

-- Do away with all loyalty oaths.

-- Capture one or both of the political parties in the United States.

-- Use technical decisions of the courts to weaken basic American institutions by claiming their activities violate civil rights.

-- Get control of the schools. Use them as transmission belts for socialism and current Communist propaganda. Soften the curriculum. Get control of teachers' associations. Put the party line in textbooks.

-- Infiltrate the press. Get control of book-review assignments, editorial writing, and policy-making positions.

-- Gain control of key positions in radio, TV, and motion pictures.

-- Continue discrediting American culture by degrading all forms of artistic expression. An American Communist cell was told to "eliminate all good sculpture from parks and buildings, substitute shapeless, awkward and meaningless forms."

-- Break down cultural standards of morality by promoting pornography and obscenity in books, magazines, motion pictures, radio, and TV.

-- Present homosexuality, degeneracy and promiscuity as "normal, natural, and healthy."

-- Infiltrate the churches and replace revealed religion with "social" religion. Discredit the Bible and emphasize the need for intellectual maturity which does not need a "religious crutch."

-- Eliminate prayer or any phase of religious expression in the schools on the ground that it violates the principle of "separation of church and state."

-- Discredit the American Constitution by calling it inadequate, old-fashioned, out of step with modern needs, a hindrance to cooperation between nations on a worldwide basis.

-- Discredit the American Founding Fathers. Present them as selfish aristocrats who had no concern for the "common man."

-- Belittle all forms of American culture and discourage the teaching of American history on the ground that it was only a minor part of the "big picture."

-- Support any socialist movement to give centralized control over any part of the culture--education, social agencies, welfare programs, mental health clinics, etc.

-- Eliminate the House Committee on Un-American Activities.

-- Infiltrate and gain control of more unions.

-- Infiltrate and gain control of big business.

-- Discredit the family as an institution. Encourage promiscuity and easy divorce.

-- Emphasize the need to raise children away from the negative influence of parents. Attribute prejudices, mental blocks and retarding of children to suppressive influence of parents.

-- Create the impression that violence and insurrection are legitimate aspects of the American tradition; that students and special-interest groups should rise up and use united force to solve economic, political or social problems.

-- Internationalize the Panama Canal.

-- Repeal the Connally reservation so the United States cannot prevent the World Court from seizing jurisdiction [over domestic problems. Give the World Court jurisdiction] over nations and individuals alike.

ADDENDUM
TWO

"At what point shall we expect the approach of danger?
By what means shall we fortify against it? Shall we expect
some trans-Atlantic military giant to step the ocean, and
crush us at a blow?

Never!

All the armies of Europe, Asia, and Africa combined, …
could not by force, take a drink from the Ohio, or make a
track on the Blue Ridge, in a trial of a thousand years.

At what point then is the approach of danger to be
expected?

I answer, if it ever reach us, it must spring up amongst us.
It cannot come from abroad. If destruction be our lot, we
ourselves must be its author and finisher. As a nation of
free men, we must live through all times, or die by suicide."

Abraham Lincoln
Address before the Young Men's Lyceum
Springfield, Illinois – January 27, 1838

- - -

This is so true today and even the media has a name for it:
"Deep State." But I hope you now see that the "Deep State"
is totally controlled by the Master Conspiracy.

- - -

Notes:

Works Cited

Allen, Gary. *The Rockefeller File.* '76 Press, 1976.

Biondi, Rick, and Alex Newman. *World Federalism 101 In Their Own Words & Deeds.* 2014.

Burnham, James. *The Web of Subversion.* Western Islands, 1954. Reprinted by special arrangement from original publisher, The John Bay Company.

Estulin, Daniel. *The True Story of the Bilderberg Group.* 2005. TrineDay, 2009.

---. *Shadow Masters: How Governments and Their Intelligence Agencies are Working with Drug Dealers and Terrorists for Mutual Benefit and Profit.* TrineDay, 2010.

Gannon, Francis X. *The Biographical Dictionary of the Left.* Western Islands, 1969. 4 vols. First vol. is personally signed by the author for Robert Ott.

Griffin, G. Edward. *The Fearful Master: A Second Look at the United Nations.* Western Islands, 1964.

Jasper, William F. *Global Tyranny...Step by Step: The United Nations and the Emerging New World Order.* Western Islands, 1992.

---. *The United Nations Exposed.* The John Birch Society, 2001.

Lee, Robert W. The United Nations Conspiracy. Western Islands, 1981.

The New American Magazine. Various vols and years. Appleton, Wisconsin. Phone: 1-800-827-TRUE thenewamerican.com

Quigley, Carroll. *Tragedy and Hope: A History of the World in Our Time.* Macmillan Publishers, 1966.

Robison, John. *Proofs of a Conspiracy.* Edinburgh, 1797. The Fourth Edition with Corrections and Additions, New-York, G. Forman, 1798. Reprinted with faithfulness to the 1798 original by Western Islands, 1967.

Skousen, W. Cleon. *The Naked Capitalist: A Review and Commentary on Dr. Carroll Quigley's Book Tragedy and Hope.* 1970. Published in private edition by the reviewer, 9th printing, 1972.

Smoot, Dan. *The Invisible Government.* Dan Smoot Report, Inc. 1962. Print. First Edition. Personally signed by Dan Smoot, Federal Bureau of Investigation agent, for Robert Ott, who spent time speaking with and driving the author to interviews in the 1960s.

Thompson, Arthur R. *In the Shadows of the Deep State: A Century of Council on Foreign Relations Scheming for World Government.* The John Birch Society, 2018.*

*For further reading and understanding of what is happening today, you should buy this book by Arthur Thompson. I recommend you buy it now for deeper reading to your children and grandchildren.

You can purchase it from the online bookstore and the phone number listed below:

For Information and Purchasing of some of these out of mainstream print titles, please contact

Western Islands (publisher)
(920) 749-3780

www.shopjbs.org

A very good source for daily news on pertinent issues is TheNewAmerican.com. Access this site and sign up for their free "Top Daily Headlines" sent to your email address. This email is not overwhelming, giving you the five top headlines of the day with background information rarely seen on other sites.

Also, please consider a subscription to *The New American* magazine. It is only 49 dollars a year for 26 magazines a year.

You can subscribe at
www.jbs.org

www.ingramcontent.com/pod-product-compliance
Lightning Source LLC
Chambersburg PA
CBHW020522030426
42337CB00011B/518